FINDING FREEDOM
IN CHRIST

Breakthrough

A STUDY IN GALATIANS

BARB ROOSE

Abingdon Women | Nashville

Breakthrough
Finding Freedom in Christ
Leader Guide

Copyright © 2021 Abingdon Press
All rights reserved.

ISBN 978-1-7910-1424-7

21 22 23 24 25 26 27 28 29 30 — 10 9 8 7 6 5 4 3 2 1
MANUFACTURED IN THE UNITED STATES OF AMERICA

Contents

About the Author

Barb Roose is a popular speaker and author who is passionate about teaching women to live beautifully strong and courageous in spite of their fears so that they can experience God's great adventure of faith and purpose for their lives. Barb enjoys teaching and encouraging women at conferences and events across the country, as well as internationally. She is the author of the Bible studies *Breakthrough: Finding Freedom in Christ*, *Surrendered: Letting Go and Living Like Jesus*, *I'm Waiting God: Finding Blessing in God's Delays*, *Joshua: Winning the Worry Battle*, and *Beautiful Already: Reclaiming God's Perspective on Beauty* and the books *Surrendered: 40 Devotions to Help You Let Go and Live Like Jesus*, *Winning the Worry Battle: Life Lessons from the Book of Joshua*, and *Enough Already: Winning Your Ugly Struggle with Beauty*. She also writes a regular blog at BarbRoose.com and hosts the *Better Together* podcast. Previously Barb was executive director of ministry at CedarCreek Church in Perrysburg, Ohio, where she served on staff for fourteen years and co-led the annual Fabulous Women's Conference that reached more than ten thousand women over five years. Barb is the proud mother of three adult daughters and lives in Northwest Ohio.

Follow Barb:

  @barbroose

  @barbroose

  Facebook.com/barbararoose

Blog BarbRoose.com
(check here for event dates and booking information)

Introduction

Have you ever felt like there's a long list of rules you have to follow in order to be a "good Christian," and you always seem to be breaking one of them? Perhaps you feel like you're just one mistake or sin away from God sending you a big "whammy." Or maybe you're just tired of trying to measure up. Whether you grew up in church and were there every time the doors were open, attended church only on Christmas and Easter, or never darkened the door of a church until recently, you might be able to relate to one or more of those feelings. The truth is, many of us have been shaped by the idea that, in order to please God, we have to jump through religious hoops—what I call the To-Do, Do-More, and Do-Better hoops. So if that's you, you're not alone!

As you lead a group of women through this study in Galatians, I pray that you'll discover together as I did that *God's love for me is based on His perfect promises, not my performance.* Whether that's a new concept or one you've known for years yet still struggle to live by, this study will help you to stop jumping through hoops and embrace the life-changing freedom of the gospel of grace!

About the Participant Book

Before the first session, you will want to distribute copies of the participant workbook to the members of your group. Be sure to communicate that they are to complete the first week of readings before your first group session. For each week there is a Scripture memory verse and five readings or lessons that combine study of Scripture with personal reflection and application. On average, each lesson can be completed in about twenty to thirty minutes. Completing these readings each week will prepare the women for the discussion and activities of the group session.

About This Leader Guide

As you gather each week with the members of your group, you will have the opportunity to watch a video, discuss and respond to what you're learning, and pray together. You will need access to a television and a DVD player with working remotes. Or, if you prefer, you may purchase streaming video files at www.Cokesbury.com, or you may access the videos for this study and other Abingdon Women Bible studies on AmplifyMedia.com through an individual or church membership.

Creating a warm and inviting atmosphere will help make the women feel welcome. Although optional, you might consider providing snacks and drinks or coffee for your first meeting and inviting group members to rotate in bringing refreshments each week.

This leader guide and the video lessons will be your primary tools for leading each group session. In this book you will find outlines for six group sessions, each formatted for either a 60-minute or 90-minute group session:

60-Minute Format

Leader Prep (Before the Session)	
Welcome and Opening Prayer	5 minutes
Icebreaker	5 minutes
Video	20 minutes
Group Discussion	25 minutes
Closing Prayer	5 minutes

90-Minute Format

Leader Prep (Before the Session)	
Welcome and Opening Prayer	5-10 minutes
Icebreaker	5 minutes
Video	20 minutes
Group Discussion	35 minutes
Deeper Conversation	15 minutes
Closing Prayer	5 minutes

As you can see, the 90-minute format is identical to the 60-minute format but allows more time for the welcome/opening prayer and group discussion plus a Deeper Conversation exercise for small groups. Feel free to adapt or modify either of these formats, as well as the individual segments and activities, in any way to meet the specific needs and preferences of your group.

Here is a brief overview of the elements included in both formats:

Leader Prep (Before the Session)

For your preparation prior to the group session, this section provides an Overview of the week's biblical theme, the week's Surrender Principle, key Scriptures, and a list of materials and equipment needed. Be sure to review this section, as well as read through the *entire* session outline, before your group time in order to plan and prepare. If you choose, you also may find it helpful to watch the video segment in advance.

Welcome and Opening Prayer (5-10 minutes, depending on session length)

Create a warm, welcoming environment as the women are gathering before the session begins, whether meeting in person or online. If meeting in person, consider lighting one or more candles, providing coffee or other refreshments, and/or playing worship music. (Bring an iPod, smartphone, or tablet and a portable speaker if desired.) Be sure to provide nametags if the women do not know one another or you have new participants in your group. When you are ready to begin, open the group in prayer before you begin your time. If meeting online, welcome each participant as she joins and encourage the women to talk informally until you are ready to open the group in prayer.

You also may find it helpful to read aloud the week's Overview found in the Leader Prep section if not all group members have completed their homework.

Icebreaker (5 minutes)

Use the icebreaker to briefly engage the women in the topic while helping them feel comfortable with one another.

Video (20 minutes)

Next, watch the week's video segment together. Be sure to direct participants to the Video Viewer Guide in the participant workbook, which they may complete as they watch the video. (Answers are provided on page 63 of this guide and page 208 in the participant workbook.)

Group Discussion (25-35 minutes, depending on session length)

After watching the video, choose from the questions provided to facilitate group discussion (questions are provided for both the video segment and the participant workbook material). For the participant workbook portion, you may choose to read aloud the discussion points or express them in your own words; then use one or more of the questions that follow to guide your conversation.

Note that more material is provided than you will have time to include. Before the session, select what questions you want to ask, putting a check mark beside them in your book. Reflect on each question and make some notes in the margins to share during your discussion time. Page references are provided for those questions that relate to specific questions or activities in the participant workbook. For these questions, invite group members to turn in their books to the pages indicated. Participants will need Bibles in order to look up various supplementary Scriptures.

Depending on the number of women in your group and the level of their participation, you may not have time to cover everything you have selected, and that is okay. Rather than attempting to bulldoze through, follow the Spirit's lead and be open to where the Spirit takes the conversation. Remember that your role is not to have all the answers but to encourage discussion and sharing.

Deeper Conversation (15 minutes)

If your group is meeting for 90 minutes, use this exercise for deeper sharing in small groups, dividing into groups of two or three. This is a time for women to share more intimately and build connections with one another. (Encourage the women to break into different groups each week.) Give a two-minute warning before time is up so that the groups may wrap up their discussion.

Closing Prayer (5 minutes)

Close by leading the group in prayer. If you'd like, invite the women to briefly name prayer requests. To get things started, you might share a personal request of your own. As women share their requests, model for the group by writing each request in your participant workbook, indicating that you will remember to pray for them during the week.

As the study progresses, you might encourage members to participate in the Closing Prayer by praying out loud for each other and the requests given. Ask the women to volunteer to pray for specific requests, or have each woman pray for the woman on her right or left. Make sure nametags are visible so that group members do not feel awkward if they do not remember someone's name.

Before You Begin

Can I tell you just how happy that I am that you're taking this *Breakthrough* journey with me? It doesn't matter where you come from or what you've been through, you can know and trust that God is with you and for you. Wherever you need a breakthrough, God has already promised freedom and desires to give it to you. Finding freedom in Christ will bless and transform your own life, and you'll be a shining light of God's hope and glory to the world around you!

Blessings,

Barb

Leader Helps

Preparing for the Sessions

- Decide whether you will use the 60-minute or 90-minute format. Be sure to communicate dates and times to participants in advance.

- Ensure that participants receive their workbooks at least one week before your first session and instruct them to complete the first week's readings. If you have the phone numbers or email addresses of your group members, send out a reminder and a welcome.

- Check out your meeting space before each group session (or set up a virtual meeting and share the link). Make sure the room is ready. Do you have enough chairs? Do you have the equipment and supplies you need? (See the list of materials needed in each session outline.)

- Pray for your group and each group member by name. Ask God to work in the life of every woman in your group.

- Read and complete the week's readings in the participant workbook and review the session outline in the leader guide. Select the discussion points and questions you want to cover and make some notes in the margins to share in your discussion time.

Leading the Sessions

- Personally welcome and greet each woman as she arrives (whether in person or online). You might want to have a sign-up list for the women to record their names and contact information.

- At the start of each session, ask the women to turn off or silence their cell phones (or eliminate other distractions if meeting online).

- Always start on time. Honor the time of those who are punctual.

- Encourage everyone to participate fully, but don't put anyone on the spot. Be prepared to offer a personal example or answer if no one else responds at first.
- Communicate the importance of completing the weekly readings and participating in group discussion.
- Facilitate but don't dominate. Remember that if you talk most of the time, group members may tend to listen rather than to engage. Your task is to encourage conversation and keep the discussion moving.
- If someone monopolizes the conversation, kindly thank her for sharing and ask if anyone else has any insights.
- Try not to interrupt, judge, or minimize anyone's comments or input.
- Remember that you are not expected to be the expert or have all the answers. Acknowledge that all of you are on this journey together, with the Holy Spirit as your leader and guide. If issues or questions arise that you don't feel equipped to handle or answer, talk with the pastor or a staff member at your church.
- Don't rush to fill the silence. If no one speaks right away, it's okay to wait for someone to answer. After a moment, ask, "Would anyone be willing to share?" If no one responds, try asking the question again a different way—or offer a brief response and ask if anyone has anything to add.
- Encourage good discussion, but don't be timid about calling time on a particular question and moving ahead. Part of your responsibility is to keep the group on track. If you decide to spend extra time on a given question or activity, consider skipping or spending less time on another question or activity in order to stay on schedule.
- End on time. If you are running over, give members the opportunity to leave if they need to. Then wrap up as quickly as you can.
- Thank the women for coming and let them know you're looking forward to seeing them next time.
- Be prepared for some women to want to hang out and talk at the end. If you need everyone to leave by a certain time, communicate this at the beginning of the group session. If you are meeting in a church during regularly scheduled activities, be aware of nursery closing times.

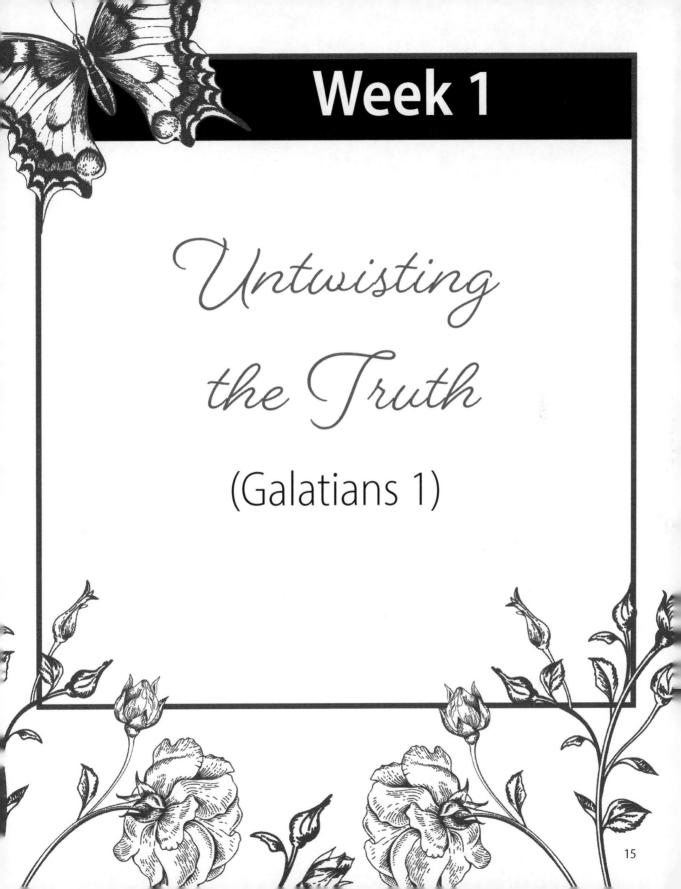

Untwisting the Truth

(Galatians 1)

Leader Prep (Before the Session)

Overview

Throughout this study, we will explore what it means to have freedom in Christ. This week, we started with Jesus's own words as He announced His ministry—words that spoke specifically to setting people free. We studied Galatians 1, in which the apostle Paul shares his own story of breakthrough with Jesus and implores the Galatian church to remember that they cannot earn or work for their freedom—that salvation in Jesus is something to be received, not earned. Paul was distressed and needed to correct the Galatians. They had turned away from the gospel. Rather than embrace the hope in Christ, the forgiveness of their sins, and the promise of eternal life, some Galatian believers weakened their connection to what they once believed by introducing additional requirements. We can relate to losing our connection to Jesus at times as we fall prey to lies or legalism and despair. But God never gives up on us! As we learned this week, the gospel is based on God's perfect promises, not our performance. Praise God!

Freedom Principle #1

The gospel is based on God's perfect promises, not our performance.

Key Scriptures

Jesus gave his life for our sins, just as God our Father planned, in order to rescue us from this evil world in which we live.

(Galatians 1:4)

[18] *"The Spirit of the LORD is upon me,*
    for he has anointed me to bring Good News to the poor.

He has sent me to proclaim that captives will be released,
  that the blind will see,
that the oppressed will be set free,
  [19] and that the time of the LORD's favor has come."

(Luke 4:18-19)

"For this is how God loved the world: He gave his one and only Son, so that everyone who believes in him will not perish but have eternal life.

(John 3:16)

For everyone has sinned; we all fall short of God's glorious standard.

(Romans 3:23)

Salvation is not a reward for the good things we have done, so none of us can boast about it.

(Ephesians 2:9)

What You Will Need

- *Breakthrough* DVD and DVD player, or equipment to stream the video online
- Bible and *Breakthrough* participant workbook for reference
- Markerboard or chart paper and markers (optional)
- Stick-on name tags and markers (optional)
- iPod, smartphone, or tablet and portable speaker (optional)

Session Outline

Welcome and Opening Prayer (5-10 minutes, depending on session length)

In order to create a warm, welcoming environment as the women are gathering before the session begins, consider lighting one or more candles, providing coffee or other refreshments, and/or playing worship music. (Bring an iPod, smartphone, or tablet and a portable speaker if desired.) Be sure to provide nametags if the women do not know one another or you have new participants in your group. Then, when you are ready to begin, open the group in prayer.

If meeting online, welcome each participant as she joins and encourage the women to talk informally until you are ready to open the group in prayer.

Icebreaker (5 minutes)

Invite the women to share short responses to the following question:

- If you had an easy button to break free from something in your life in an instant, what would that something be?

Video (20 minutes)

Play the Week 1 video segment. Invite participants to complete the Video Viewer Guide for Week 1 in the participant workbook as they watch (page 42).

Group Discussion (25-35 minutes, depending on session length)

Note: More material is provided than you will have time to include. Before the session, select what you want to cover.

Video Discussion Questions
- Read aloud Luke 4:18-21. Barb shared that Jesus proclaimed that His whole ministry is about setting people free. When you hear this Scripture passage, what do you think Jesus meant when He said He came to set the captives free?
- Do you believe that Jesus can set you free? Why or why not? How does Jesus set us free?
- When have you experienced prisons of your past, your problems, or your pain? What was that like? What were the lies the enemy whispered to you in those seasons?
- If the gospel is about receiving from God rather than following rules, why do you think we sometimes fall back into a prison of trying to do all the right things instead of living freely in Christ?
- Have you ever been caught up in any of the three legalism hoops—To-Do, Do-More, or Do-Better? What was that experience like? How did you get out of the cycle?

Participant Workbook Discussion Questions
1. On Day 1, Barb introduced this week's reading by explaining that Paul wrote Galatians to bring some clarity to the question: What is the gospel? The believers in Galatia were saying and doing things in conflict with the truth of the gospel and had begun to distract and divide the church. (Day 1)

- How would you describe the gospel to someone who has never heard about Jesus?
- Historically, what are some ways that believers have gotten confused about the core of the gospel and maybe even said and done things in conflict with the truth of the gospel?
- What do you think of when you hear the term *church hurt*? Have you ever experienced emotional, spiritual, or abusive wounds within a Christian community? (Refer to page 15.) Why is it so important to center ourselves around the gospel and nothing else?

2. Before Paul met Jesus, he persecuted early believers—having them stoned, thrown in jail, and even put to death. Because of his past, Paul's qualifications for preaching the gospel would be brought into question over and over. But Paul was called by God. His confidence to teach and preach boldly was fueled by living in God's grace. Paul didn't hide from his past. He could have been ashamed of who he was, but instead he allowed the power of the gospel to rescue, restore, and redeem where he'd come from and what he'd done. (Day 1)

   - Are there any reasons you feel unqualified to be used by God? (page 17)
   - Read 1 Corinthians 15:9-10. How does Paul describe himself in relation to the other apostles? What does Paul reveal about his past? (page 17) Why is Paul saying he is able to preach the gospel now?
   - Read aloud this week's Memory Verse, Galatians 1:4. How would you say that passage in your own words? When have you felt Jesus rescue you?

3. The gospel is God's rescue of humanity as we willingly surrender our lives to Him so that He can renew our souls, redeem our mistakes, and restore us to wholeness. At the core of the gospel is God's desire to give and our willingness to receive. (Day 2)

   - Read aloud Romans 3:23; 6:23; 2 Corinthians 5:17; and Ephesians 2:10. What do these verses tell us about the grace of God? What do they say about what we receive? (pages 20–21)

- What does it mean that God can renew our souls, redeem our mistakes, and restore us to wholeness? How have you experienced this renewal, redemption, and restoration in your own life?
- What are some of the "extras" we add to the gospel—whether knowingly or unknowingly? Why do you think it can be a struggle to accept the grace of the gospel as it is?
- When you look at the Gospel Wheel, which aspect of God's activity is hardest for you to receive? Why? (page 22)

4. Confusion about the gospel happens when we stop believing that receiving is enough to make us right with God. It is not the gospel of Jesus if it is something to be earned, worked for, or to-do listed. The gospel is based on God's perfect promises, not our performance. (Day 2)

- Read Galatians 1:3-4. How would you summarize the gospel of grace message in your own words? (page 20)
- Is there anything you feel (or have felt) you must do to earn or keep your salvation? (page 23)
- Why do you need to remember the power of the gospel in your life *each day*? (page 23) What are some ways we can intentionally remember the power of the gospel at work in our lives each day?
- How has the gospel given you purpose and positioned you for a life of adventure with Jesus? What situations in your life (past or present) demonstrate the adventures that the gospel has brought into your life? (page 21)

5. In Galatians, we see that Paul is distressed because the believers have turned away from the gospel. Rather than embrace the hope in Christ, the forgiveness of their sins, and the promise of eternal life, some Galatian believers dropped their connection to what they once believed.... If you've been a part of church for more than a few years, chances are you've seen some human-related shortcomings that hurt not only others but also the heart of God. However, the power of the gospel is and always will be greater than our human failings, which is exactly why we need the gospel. (Day 3)

- Read Galatians 1:6-9. What are people turning away from? What are they following after? What does Paul mean in verse 7? (page 25)
- What's an issue within your church or denomination that has created conflict? How does this conflict impact how you feel when you're at church or trying to stay engaged in your faith? (page 27)
- What aspects of who God is have you allowed to get twisted, either through your life experience or the influence of others? (page 28)
- What lies about yourself have you believed, either through your life experience or the influence of others? (page 28)

6. The believers Paul was writing to in Galatia had begun to practice what is called *legalism*. Legalism is when we're focused on what we are doing for God rather than on what we receive from God. Some legalism is motivated by not feeling we're enough for God—so we need to try harder or pray harder or read the Bible more often to earn God's affection. Another kind of legalism is driven by pride. When we think that God loves us because we've earned it, we're prone to boast or brag. (Day 4)

- Have you ever struggled with legalism? If so, how? What are some legalistic rules that you thought you needed to live by?
- Read Ephesians 2:9. How did you summarize this verse? (page 31) What does this verse say about working for salvation?
- Read Matthew 12:1-2. How did Jesus challenge legalism?

7. One of the enticements of legalism is the temptation to judge our spiritual growth or transformation according to our actions. Sometimes, we get distracted or discouraged, so we don't see where God is working in our lives. At other times, we don't see where God is working until we share our story with others. It's in our story that we see God's power working through us, not for our glory but for God's alone. (Day 5)

- Why do you think Paul told his whole story in Galatians chapter 1?
- Review the highlights from the story of Zacchaeus in Luke 19:1-10. What is Zacchaeus's story? What are three ways you can see God at work in Zacchaeus's life even though it's not spelled out in the story? (page 39) How is a story like his a powerful witness to what God can do?

- How could your story of walking with Jesus help lead someone to a breakthrough of their own?

Deeper Conversation (15 minutes)

Divide into smaller groups of 2-3 for deeper conversation. (Encourage the women to break into different groups each week.) If you'd like, before the session, write on a markerboard or chart paper the question below. You also could also do this in the form of a handout.

- Look at the six kinds of ah-ha moments on page 41. Choose one example from your reflection to share with the group. When have you noticed in big or small ways that God is changing you from the inside out?

Closing Prayer (5 minutes)

Close the session by taking personal prayer requests from group members and leading the group in prayer. As you progress to later weeks in the study, you might encourage members to participate by praying out loud for each other and the requests given.

Freedom Fighters

(Galatians 2)

Leader Prep (Before the Session)

Overview

This week, we looked to Jesus as the only one who can save us, justify us, and bring us freedom. Jesus came to earth to show us what God is like. While He walked among humanity, He was criticized and accused by religious leaders. Not everyone in Jesus's family believed that that He was the Messiah. He allowed Himself to be beaten and crucified by the very people He came to save.

When we don't see the gospel as enough in our lives, we diminish Jesus's sacrifice. When we wear ourselves out worrying about whether we're reading our Bible enough, serving enough, giving enough, or praying enough like a "good Christian," we treat God's grace as meaningless.

On the other hand, we live fully in the grace of God when we wake up each day and say, "God, I am ready to live for You today because of the grace You have given me." And we live fully in the beautiful grace of God each time we reject the tyranny of rule-keeping and cherish the personal, life-giving relationship we have with God because of what Jesus Christ did for us.

Freedom Principle #2

A relationship with God means that we receive from Him rather than follow rules for Him.

Key Scriptures

My old self has been crucified with Christ. It is no longer I who live, but Christ lives in me. So I live in this earthly body by trusting in the Son of God, who loved me and gave himself for me.

(Galatians 2:20)

"Don't misunderstand why I have come. I did not come to abolish the law of Moses or the writings of the prophets. No, I came to accomplish their purpose."

(Matthew 5:17)

[20]You have died with Christ, and he has set you free from the spiritual powers of this world. So why do you keep on following the rules of the world, such as, [21] "Don't handle! Don't taste! Don't touch!"? [22] Such rules are mere human teachings about things that deteriorate as we use them. [23] These rules may seem wise because they require strong devotion, pious self-denial, and severe bodily discipline. But they provide no help in conquering a person's evil desires.

(Colossians 2:20-23)

[15]"We who are Jews by birth and not sinful Gentiles [16] know that a person is not justified by the works of the law, but by faith in Jesus Christ. So we, too, have put our faith in Christ Jesus that we may be justified by faith in Christ and not by the works of the law, because by the works of the law no one will be justified."

(Galatians 2:15-16 NIV)

Therefore, if anyone is in Christ, the new creation has come: The old has gone and the new is here!

(2 Corinthians 5:17 NIV)

What You Will Need

- *Breakthrough* DVD and DVD player, or equipment to stream the video online
- Bible and *Breakthrough* participant workbook for reference
- Markerboard or chart paper and markers (optional)
- Stick-on name tags and markers (optional)
- iPod, smartphone, or tablet and portable speaker (optional)

Session Outline

Welcome and Opening Prayer (5-10 minutes, depending on session length)

In order to create a warm, welcoming environment as the women are gathering before the session begins, consider lighting one or more candles, providing coffee or other refreshments, and/or playing worship music. (Bring an iPod, smartphone, or tablet and a portable speaker if desired.) Be sure to provide nametags if the women do not know one another or you have new participants in your group. Then, when you are ready to begin, open the group in prayer.

If meeting online, welcome each participant as she joins and encourage the women to talk informally until you are ready to open the group in prayer.

Icebreaker (5 minutes)

Invite the women to share short responses to the following question:

- Which hoop do you tend to jump through most often? To-do, Do-More, or Do-Better?

Video (20 minutes)

Play the Week 2 video segment. Invite participants to complete the Video Viewer Guide for Week 2 in the participant workbook as they watch (page 74).

Group Discussion (25-35 minutes, depending on session length)

Note: More material is provided than you will have time to include. Before the session, select what you want to cover.

Video Discussion Questions
- What do you think of when you hear the word *hypocrisy*? What images does it conjure up for you?
- Do you ever feel that you have to earn God's learn or approval? Why do you think it is such a hard thing for us to comprehend that God loves us regardless of our behavior?
- What do you think of the terms "good Christian" and "bad Christian"? How would you describe each?
- Have you ever struggled against lies that suggest you're not good enough, reminding you of your past sins or failures and keeping you from living in freedom?
- When have you tried to blaze a path to your own righteousness, trying to do more or be better in your own strength?

Participant Workbook Discussion Questions
1. The Big Idea for Day 1 is that *Grace brings people together, but rules distract and divide.* This is evidenced by Paul's three teaching points in Galatians 2:

1) what happened at the Jerusalem Council (recorded in Acts 15); 2) how church leaders navigated a tough issue by agreeing together that the gospel is based on God's perfect promises, not personal performance; and 3) the idea that a relationship with God begins with receiving from God rather than following rules for God. (Day 1)

- How have you seen grace bring people together? When have you seen rules distract and divide communities of faith?
- According to Galatians 2, what was going on in the Galatian church that Paul needed to write to them about?
- If the gospel is based on God's perfect promises, why do you think we often feel we need to perform in our faith as if playing a role in a play?

2. There are a lot of hot-button issues in the church today. Depending on your background or denomination, you might be dealing with a few of those issues now.... If there ever was a hill to die on, this is it: the centrality of the gospel. Just as Paul and the leaders in Jerusalem refused to give in, even for a single moment, we too must stand strong on the gospel. Nowhere do we read that Paul and the other leaders were mean, disrespectful, violent, or disparaging toward the false teachers—only that they preserved the truth of the gospel. (Day 1)

- Is there any secondary issue at your church distracting you these days? If so, what is it? What are some clues that you might be overly distracted? (page 51)
- What would it look like for you to live out the gospel even though there might be distractions around you? (page 51)
- Read aloud this week's Memory Verse, Galatians 2:20. How would you say this passage in your own words? How does this verse help us when we're confused about how to live out the gospel of Jesus?

3. The Big Idea for Day 2 is that *Jesus fulfilled the law for our freedom.* Jesus didn't come to get rid of the law. After all, the law reflects God's perfect and sovereign character. Jesus came to fulfill or satisfy the requirements of the law that God's people could not do on their own. (Day 2)

- Read Matthew 5:17. What do you think Jesus meant by saying that He came to accomplish or fulfill the law? (page 55)
- Read Hebrews 9:13-14. What is the difference between animal sacrifices and Jesus's sacrifice? (page 54)
- How does the law reflect God's perfect character?

4. Though our culture and customs are different than those of the Jewish and Gentile believers of Paul's day, we still struggle with thinking that we need to follow rules in order to please God. (Day 2)

- What rules do you think you need to follow in order to please God?
- Read Colossians 2:20-23. What does this verse say about rule-following? What does it mean to have "died with Christ" and to be "set free from the spiritual powers of this world"?

5. By definition, hypocrisy is the result of when our behavior doesn't match our stated beliefs. No one likes to be called a hypocrite, but we all make mistakes. We lie, even though we believe that lying is wrong. We are unloving, even though God calls us to love. We're human and, at times, we can be hypocrites. (Day 3)

- Read Galatians 2:12. What, specifically, did Paul confront Peter about? When and why did Peter change his behavior? (page 58)
- Read Galatians 2:13-14. How did Peter's hypocrisy influence others? What question did Paul ask Peter? (page 58)
- How are legalism and hypocrisy like dynamite and a match?
- Peter was afraid of breaking rules, so much so that he wasn't experiencing freedom in Christ. What kind of fears and rules keep you from living God's best for you?

6. In order to be justified, we have to recognize our need for God's rescue. One of the criticisms. . . from non-Christians is that many Christians seem to think that they are better than everyone else. Justification reminds us that we owed God a debt of sin that we couldn't pay. (Day 4)

- How would you describe justification in Christ to someone?
- Read Galatians 2:15-16. Share your rewrite of verse 16 on page 63. How would you explain Paul's writing in your own words?
- Have you ever heard the criticism that many Christians seem to think they're better than everyone else? Is this a fair criticism? Why or why not?
- Why is justification a cornerstone of the gospel?

7. When Paul writes that our old life has been crucified with Christ, he means exactly that. Picture Jesus hanging on the cross with your sins, failures, shortcomings, and struggles nailed to the cross. He died and took all of that with Him. Not only that, but when we realize that Christ lives in us, we're assured that the power of the gospel of grace, which rescues us, continues to work in our lives each day whether we've been saved for five minutes or fifty years. (Day 5)

- What is your before, during, and after story of meeting Jesus? Describe your old self before you placed your faith in Jesus Christ. At what point did you realize that you need Christ in your life? Describe what happened. (page 67–68)
- Describe a moment in the past or present when you've seen Christ at work in your life and knew the gospel of grace was alive in you. (page 68)
- Read 2 Corinthians 5:17. Do you feel like a new creation because of what Jesus has done on your behalf? What, if anything, is keeping you from living in new creation freedom?
- When have you experienced freedom in Christ and really felt it in your spirit?

Deeper Conversation (15 minutes)

Divide into smaller groups of 2-3 for deeper conversation. (Encourage the women to break into different groups each week.) If you'd like, before the session, write on a markerboard or chart paper the following questions. You could also do this in the form of a handout.

- Look at your ah-ha moments from the week and share about one of them.
- What spiritual breakthrough are you praying for right now?

Closing Prayer (5 minutes)

Close the session by taking personal prayer requests from group members and leading the group in prayer. As you progress to later weeks in the study, you might encourage members to participate by praying out loud for each other and the requests given.

Video

↳ + still make
← we can all/ mistakes.
- repents resists

- eyes in hula-hoop
- receive rules

• prison of perfection
• hypocrisy - destraction
  + devastation
• Lu.6 - a tree - good + bad
  fruit
• dream in Acts 10
• Acts 10:28 - Peter
  "   "   34-35 - no favoritism
• God's gospel of grace
• a temperature ✓ on my heart

• our memory verse
  Gal 2:20 my old self
  has been crucified
• where let go ?

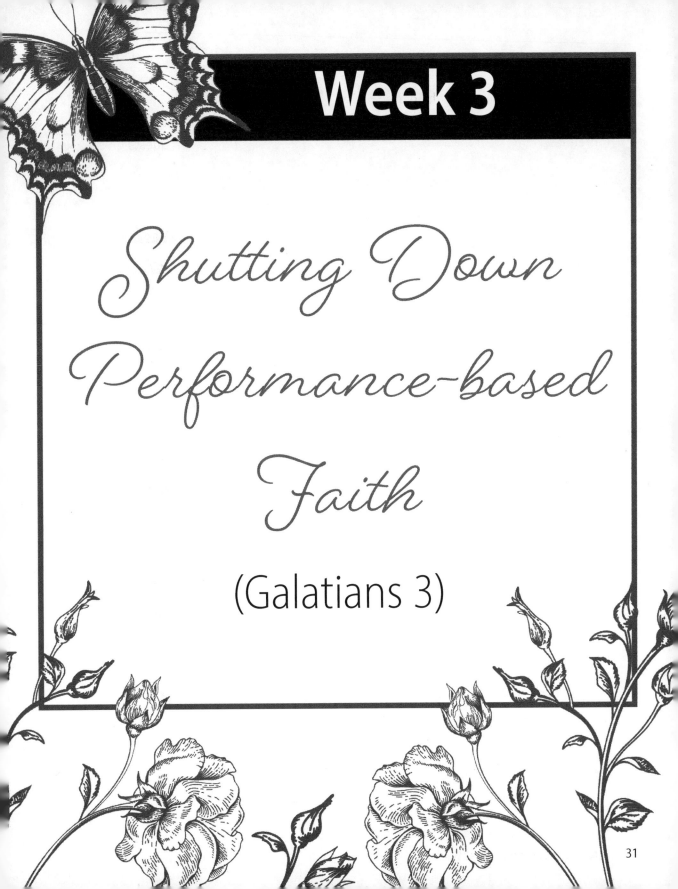

Week 3

Shutting Down Performance-based Faith

(Galatians 3)

Leader Prep (Before the Session)

Overview

In our study this week, Paul expands upon the reasons why the law wasn't the remedy that our hearts needed. Like a recipe, the law itself is a good thing, but because of sin, following the law didn't guarantee perfection. In the study, we also saw the connections between the old covenant and the new covenant and why the law was needed between them. We studied the vision Paul cast on a topic that our world needs now more than ever: *unity.* And we considered Paul's reminders to the Galatians about the gospel, highlighting or celebrating their oneness in Christ. His words remind us that we are all children of God, which provides an opportunity for us to discuss an important question for all Christians today: *Are we truly seeing every believer as an equal heir to God's promises?* Talking about our differences isn't easy, especially when it concerns our different colors and cultures. However, we want to establish a foundation that creates opportunities for us to embrace the same posture as the Acts 2 community, which saw incredible growth (Acts 2:47).

Freedom Principle #3

Your freedom in Christ cannot be shaken or taken away by anyone who chooses not to live like Christ.

Key Scriptures

So in Christ Jesus you are all children of God through faith.
(Galatians 3:26 NIV)

[16]God is love. . . . [18] Such love has no fear, because perfect love expels all fear. If we are afraid, it is for fear of punishment, and this shows that we have not fully experienced his perfect love.

(1 John 4:16b, 18)

24 Oh, what a miserable person I am! Who will free me from this life that is dominated by sin and death? 25 Thank God! The answer is in Jesus Christ our Lord.

(Romans 7:24-25a)

14 Because God's children are human beings—made of flesh and blood—the Son also became flesh and blood. For only as a human being could he die, and only by dying could he break the power of the devil, who had the power of death. 15 Only in this way could he set free all who have lived their lives as slaves to the fear of dying.

(Hebrews 2:14-15)

By this everyone will know that you are my disciples, if you love one another."

(John 13:35 NIV)

What You Will Need

- *Breakthrough* DVD and DVD player, or equipment to stream the video online
- Bible and *Breakthrough* participant workbook for reference
- Markerboard or chart paper and markers (optional)
- Stick-on name tags and markers (optional)
- iPod, smartphone, or tablet and portable speaker (optional)

Session Outline

Welcome and Opening Prayer (5-10 minutes, depending on session length)

In order to create a warm, welcoming environment as the women are gathering before the session begins, consider lighting one or more candles, providing coffee or other refreshments, and/or playing worship music. (Bring an iPod, smartphone, or tablet and a portable speaker if desired.) Be sure to provide nametags if the women do not know one another or you have new participants in your group. Then, when you are ready to begin, open the group in prayer.

If meeting online, welcome each participant as she joins and encourage the women to talk informally until you are ready to open the group in prayer.

Icebreaker (5 minutes)

Invite the women to share short responses to the following question:

- What is an injustice in the world or a division in the body of Christ that breaks your heart?

Video (20 minutes)

Play the Week 3 video segment. Invite participants to complete the Video Viewer Guide for Week 3 in the participant workbook as they watch (page 109).

Group Discussion (25-35 minutes, depending on session length)

Note: More material is provided than you will have time to include. Before the session, select what you want to cover.

Video Discussion Questions
- How have you seen Christ-followers work on perfecting disagreement and distrust rather than unity?
- What is the unifying message of those who follow Jesus?
- What are some ways in Scripture that you see justice as a reflection of God's heart?
- How does the gospel transform, transmit, and transcend?
- What do you think is required for unity among believers?

Participant Workbook Discussion Questions
1. Most of us have a recipe of rules for the Christian life based on what we think a good Christian looks like. Our recipes may include a few different ingredients depending on our particular denomination. (Day 1)

    - Share your recipe for the Christian life. (page 78)
    - Is your Christian-life "recipe" a formula or a guide? (page 79) Have you ever confused the two? What was that experience like?
    - How do spiritual practices (ingredients) align us with God's heart and fuel us for peace and power?

2. Paul's words in Galatians 3:1-5 remind us that we must be vigilant in *thinking about our thinking*. We have to be clear about what our beliefs are so that we can live them out and be aware of when others pressure us to change our beliefs. (Day 1)

- Read Galatians 3:1-5. What does it mean to have the indwelling of the Holy Spirt? How have you seen God's Holy Spirit at work in your life? (page 82)
- Have you ever experienced someone challenging your beliefs? What was that like? Were you able to hold on to your beliefs? Explain.
- When have you tried to become perfect on your own effort? How did that go? How can we let our faith practices be a guide and not fall into the trap of making a recipe of them?
- How can we become vigilant in our thinking about our thinking—being clear about our beliefs?

3. The Big Idea for Day 2 is that *When God makes a promise, He doesn't need our help to keep it.* The covenants with Abram, Moses, and the new covenant through Jesus Christ reveal to us that God's promises demonstrate God's faithfulness. (Day 2)

- Read Genesis 15:6 and Romans 4:9-10. Reflect on Abram's belief alone, without any other requirements. Is there a place in your life that you need to choose to believe God without making it more complicated? (page 84)
- How does God's covenant with Abraham reflect the gospel of grace as it relates to us? (page 85)
- Have you ever tried to "help" God keep a promise or tried to "help" God achieve something you were praying for? Share about that experience and the result.

4. Jesus came and died to so that you could experience eternal freedom from sin as well as freedom from wherever you come from or whatever you've been through. (Day 3)

- What comes to your mind and heart when you hear this statement?
- What does it mean to need freedom from your past, pain, problems, fears, or failures? Why do those things keep us bound up?
- Read John 8:36. What does it mean to be free? Do you believe that you are free? Do you live like you are free? Why or why not?

5. Two truths help us understand our need to read and understand both the Old and New Testaments: 1) God's love for us has never changed; and 2) Our love for sin hasn't changed either. The [Old Testament] law directed people's actions but couldn't change their hearts and minds, and the law certainly didn't have power to help them overcome the fear, self-centeredness, pride, and more that kept them in violation of the law. Of course, someone could endeavor to follow the law and feel a sense of satisfaction or even superiority, but that feeling would only last until the next moment when they had to keep the next law. Just as the law demonstrates how far our hearts are from God, so the gospel guarantees that Christ draws us near through a personal relationship with Him. (Day 3)

   - Read Galatians 3:21-22. How would you summarize this passage in your own words? (page 90)
   - Read 1 John 4:16b, 18. Why can we have freedom over fear? What fears does the gospel of grace give you freedom over today? (page 92)
   - Read Psalm 119:45 and Romans 7:24-25a. How can we experience freedom from self-destruction? Why do we need freedom from self-destruction?
   - Read Hebrews 2:14-15. How can we experience freedom from the fear of death? When we think about death, we consider our mortality, but we also think about those we love. How does it comfort you knowing that the gospel can bring freedom from death not only for you but also for those you care about? (page 93)

6. One definition of unity is *a gathering of imperfect people passionately committed to something greater than themselves*. Unity is powerful because our human nature is to reject our differences and tear each other down. Lucky for us, the gospel of grace recognizes our shortcomings as human beings. As believers, we're united by the gospel that frees us to stand together and share Jesus's message with the world. Paul teaches that everyone is an equal heir to the promises of God and we are to treat each other as equal heirs. (Day 4)

   - When was the last time you felt a sense of unity or togetherness with your Bible study group, social/volunteer organization, or church? What contributed to that sense of unity? (page 95)
   - Read Galatians 3:26-29. What makes us children of God? (page 95)

- Read Colossians 3:12-14. What are the "clothing" characteristics that believers should wear? How do these qualities support an individual's contribution toward unity with other believers? (page 96)
- Why do you think Christians have always struggled and continue to struggle with unity despite the fact that we say the gospel is the center of our faith? (page 98)
- Read John 17:20-23. What was Jesus praying for? How can we be a part of answering Jesus's prayer for unity in John 17?

7. Within God's very nature is diversity, described as the *Trinity*. While the word *Trinity* isn't a word specifically mentioned in the Bible, the doctrine of the Trinity states that there is one God who eternally exists as three distinct Persons—the Father, Son, and Holy Spirit. (Day 5)

- How does God's triune nature model for us how to live in unity and celebrate our differences? What are some ways your church celebrates differences?
- What bias or harmful stereotypes within your faith community or the body of Christ in general might be preventing people who look or live differently than you do from hearing the gospel message or joining the church?

8. Knowing that God purposefully introduced different colors and cultures into the world should motivate us to embrace those who are different from us, remembering that our differences are desirable and good. (Day 5)

- What are some positives you've discovered in meeting and interacting with people of other races and nationalities? (page 103)
- If you have limited experiences to draw from, can you speculate on the kinds of things you might be missing out on? (page 104)

9. Just as Paul elevated the gospel to the Galatians in hopes that they would guard their hearts against the deceptive words of the Judaizers, so it's up to us to guard our hearts against beliefs or behaviors that would undermine the gospel by creating division between us and other believers. (Day 5)

- Read John 13:35. How does this verse apply to the way we treat others, even those who are different from us?

- Read Proverbs 31:8-9, Jeremiah 22:3, and Micah 6:8. For whom are we to speak up? What actions we are instructed to take on behalf of those who are treated unjustly? What does it mean to do justice? Love mercy? Walk humbly with God? (page 105)
- Are there any steps you need to take in order to speak up for those who don't have a voice or whose voice is not honored as it should be? If so, for whom are you feeling called to advocate, represent, or defend? If not, what is holding you back? (pages 105–106)

Deeper Conversation (15 minutes)

Divide into smaller groups of 2-3 for deeper conversation. (Encourage the women to break into different groups each week.) If you'd like, before the session, write on a markerboard or chart paper the questions below. You could also do this in the form of a handout.

- Look at the takeaways from Day 5 that you described on page 106. How do you sense God calling you to reflect God's heart for unity within diversity? What actions is God inviting you to take?
- Look at your ah-ha moments from the week and share about one of them.
- What spiritual breakthrough are you praying for right now?

Closing Prayer (5 minutes)

Close the session by taking personal prayer requests from group members and leading the group in prayer. As you progress to later weeks in the study, you might encourage members to participate by praying out loud for each other and the requests given.

Week 4

Finding Freedom

(Galatians 4)

Leader Prep (Before the Session)

Overview

In our study this week, we dug into Galatians 4, which is all about our status as sons or daughters—children of God. In Galatians 4, Paul uses the metaphor of slavery to describe how the Galatian believers' "works of the law" or legalism resulted in bondage, not freedom in their faith. The same can be true of us. We tell ourselves that if we can just live up to whatever standard that we've set for ourselves, then we'll feel free—or at least feel better. But that's not the case. Our constant striving only leads to more stress and more striving, never bringing true freedom.

Paul's concern for the Galatians was their lack of understanding regarding their identity in Christ. They allowed themselves to be drawn by the Judaizers into a dark tunnel and back into To-Do and Do-More behaviors. While frustrated and a little discouraged, Paul continues to compel them to remember the power of the gospel in their lives. That same power is available to us as we seek a breakthrough from fear to freedom.

Freedom Principle #4

Freedom in Christ is living free from fear and fully alive with joy and purpose.

Key Scriptures

Dear brothers and sisters, I plead with you to live as I do in freedom from these things, for I have become like you Gentiles—free from those laws.

(Galatians 4:12)

⁶ Though he was God,
*   he did not think of equality with God*
*   as something to cling to.*
⁷ Instead, he gave up his divine privileges;
*   he took the humble position of a slave*

and was born as a human being.
When he appeared in human form,
  ⁸ he humbled himself in obedience to God
  and died a criminal's death on a cross.
                    (Philippians 2:6-8)

Let us then approach God's throne of grace with confidence, so that we may receive mercy and find grace to help us in our time of need.

                              (Hebrews 4:16 NIV)

But now that you know God—or rather are known by God—how is it that you are turning back to those weak and miserable forces? Do you wish to be enslaved by them all over again?

                              (Galatians 4:9 NIV)

What You Will Need

- *Breakthrough* DVD and DVD player, or equipment to stream the video online
- Bible and *Breakthrough* participant workbook for reference
- Markerboard or chart paper and markers (optional)
- Stick-on name tags and markers (optional)
- iPod, smartphone, or tablet and portable speaker (optional)

Session Outline

Welcome and Opening Prayer (5-10 minutes, depending on session length)

In order to create a warm, welcoming environment as the women are gathering before the session begins, consider lighting one or more candles, providing coffee or other refreshments, and/or playing worship music. (Bring an iPod, smartphone, or tablet and a portable speaker if desired.) Be sure to provide nametags if the women do not know one another or you have new participants in your group. Then, when you are ready to begin, open the group in prayer.

If meeting online, welcome each participant as she joins and encourage the women to talk informally until you are ready to open the group in prayer.

Icebreaker (5 minutes)

Invite the women to share short responses to the following question:

- What is your favorite princess fairytale? Why?

Video (20 minutes)

Play the Week 4 video segment. Invite participants to complete the Video Viewer Guide for Week 4 in the participant workbook as they watch (page 143).

Group Discussion (25-35 minutes, depending on session length)

Note: More material is provided than you will have time to include. Before the session, select what you want to cover.

Video Discussion Questions
- Describe the feeling of being free. Now describe the feeling of being bound up in fears or sin.
- How do we know if we are living as slaves or as heirs?
- Would you say that your faith is driven by what you do or what you allow God to do in you? What is the difference?
- When have you felt free from fear and fully alive? How did you get to the place of being fully alive?

Participant Workbook Discussion Questions
1. Paul taught that faith in Christ alone is sufficient. The truth is that the law wasn't sophisticated spirituality; it was a simple, step-by-step attempt to appear more spiritual. After all, it can seem to be easier to follow steps than to fully surrender to grace, allowing the Holy Spirit to change us from the inside out. (Day 1)

   - How does surrendering to the Holy Spirit change us from the inside out?
   - When have you seen "Christian rules" become a legalistic trap, tempting us to appear more spiritual than others? What happened?
   - What helps you to recognize this trap and fully surrender to grace?

2. Jesus became a slave so that we could gain our freedom. Rather than coming to earth to make sure we were following the rules, Jesus came to make a way for us to have a relationship with God. There's no amount of legalism in the world that motivates a person to lay down his or her life for others. Only love can do that. (Day 1)

- Read Philippians 2:5-8. As you think about your attitude toward whatever you're dealing with in your life, what aspect of Jesus's example of humble servanthood challenges or inspires you today? (page 116)
- Read Galatians 4:4. According to this verse, God sent Jesus at what point in time? (page 115) What made it the right time for God to send Jesus into the world?
- When have you experienced Jesus right on time when you needed Him?

3. The gospel message is that God became one of us to free us from the sin that was destroying us because we couldn't become righteous on our own. God didn't send Jesus to save us and then mistreat us. God adopted us as His very own children with all of the rights and privileges that come with being a part of His family. (Day 2)

- What does it mean to be an heir? What does it mean to be part of God's family?
- When do you feel a connection with God? When do you feel unloved by God? (page 118)
- Read Galatians 4:6. According to this verse, what can we call God? (page 119) In what ways have you experienced God as a good father? In what ways, if any, do you struggle with this image of God?
- Read Hebrews 4:16. How are we to approach God? When we come near to God, how will He respond? (page 119) How does this truth help you to live in freedom?

4. Not only does the gospel make it possible for us to approach God as our Abba Father; it makes us the recipients of so much more. (Day 2)

- Read Galatians 4:7. What does this verse mean regarding our spiritual inheritance?
- Have you ever inherited anything? If so, what did that inherited item mean to you? (page 120)
- What part of our divine inheritance is available to us for daily use now? (See Extra Insight on page 122.)

5. There may be people in our lives who are making reckless and unwise decisions in their spiritual lives—such as skipping or avoiding church, being influenced by relationships with legalistic Christians, or reading and watching material that isn't aligned with the gospel. All of that can be difficult for us to observe; yet although we can express our best hopes for them and encourage them toward the gospel, we're not in control of others. (Day 3)

   - Read Galatians 4:9-20. What was Paul's concern for the Galatians? What was his hope for them? (page 127)
   - Is there a situation in your life where you need to let go of trying to "fix" someone's faith? (page 127)
   - If we can't fix others and the only person we can control is ourself, then we must ask ourselves, *What is my identity in Christ?* How would you answer this question? What are some true statements about who you are in Jesus that can anchor you when you might get confused about what is true?

6. The Big Idea for Day 4 is that our bad decisions, baggage, and brokenness are never too big for God's power and presence to guide us toward a life-changing breakthrough. This means that God doesn't want you to remain trapped in whatever prison of your past, pain, or problems you're stuck in because of a mistake that you've made—or even one that you're living in right now. (Day 4)

   - Review the highlights of the story of Abraham, Sarah, and Hagar. What were some bad decisions they made? What baggage did each one carry? Where did brokenness occur? How did God bring about a breakthrough?
   - What are some of *your* takeaways from the story of Abraham, Sarah, and Hagar? (page 133)
   - Read Galatians 4:28-31. Why does Paul refer to Isaac and Ishmael?
   - Have you ever tried to get God's promise on your own power and your own timeline? How did that work out for you?
   - When have you believed that your brokenness, bad decisions, and baggage were too much? Did you experience a breakthrough in that season, and if so, how?

7. When our minds are constantly in motion, filled with To-Do, Do-More, and Do-Better actions, we're not leaving God much room to speak into and adjust our thoughts, attitudes, or beliefs. One of the reasons that we have To-Do, Do-More, and Do-Better impulses to begin with is because we believe that the more we do for God, the less fear or guilt we'll have that we're disappointing Him. (Day 5)

- Do you ever get so busy doing things for God that you neglect to just be with God? What prompts you to slow down when that happens?
- How does slowing down help you hear God better?
- How busy are you physically and mentally on a regular basis? Share the results of your self-check from page 136. When you are mentally tired, how does that impact your physical, emotional, and spiritual well-being? (page 137)
- Do you set aside sufficient time for rest and renewal? If so, how do you safeguard this time? If not, what is keeping you from Sabbath rest?
- What did you learn about walking and talking? How would you like to incorporate either or both of these practices in your life?

Deeper Conversation (15 minutes)

Divide into smaller groups of 2-3 for deeper conversation. (Encourage the women to break into different groups each week.) If you'd like, before the session, write on a markerboard or chart paper the questions below. You could also do this in the form of a handout.

- Look at your ah-ha moments from the week and share about one of them.
- What spiritual breakthrough are you praying for right now?

Closing Prayer (5 minutes)

Close the session by taking personal prayer requests from group members and leading the group in prayer. Encourage members to participate by praying out loud for each other and the requests given.

Week 5

Live Free!

(Galatians 5)

Leader Prep (Before the Session)

Overview

In this week's study, we saw Paul call the Galatian believers to not only know that they are free, but also to *live* as people who are free—to experience the freedom that Jesus promised. We discovered that because of Christ's death and resurrection, we have the permanent gift of the Holy Spirit, who indwells us. We can experience the Holy Spirit continuing to transform our hearts and minds from self-righteous legalism to Spirit-driven attitudes, behaviors, and character.

Freedom Principle #5

Spiritual breakthrough is an ah-ha moment when we recognize that God is at work within us, receive what He's doing, and respond to it.

Key Scriptures

It is for freedom that Christ set you free. Stand firm, then, and do not let yourselves be burdened again by a yoke of slavery.

(Galatians 5:1 NIV)

[28] "Come to me, all you who are weary and burdened, and I will give you rest. [29] Take my yoke upon you and learn from me, for I am gentle and humble in heart, and you will find rest for your souls. [30] For my yoke is easy and my burden is light."

(Matthew 11:28-30 NIV)

You say, "I am allowed to do anything"—but not everything is good for you. You say, "I am allowed to do anything"—but not everything is beneficial.

(1 Corinthians 10:23)

I want to do what is good, but I don't. I don't want to do what is wrong, but I do it anyway.

(Romans 7:19)

"But the tax collector stood at a distance. He would not even look up to heaven, but beat his breast and said, 'God, have mercy on me, a sinner.'"

(Luke 18:13 NIV)

Therefore, there is now no condemnation for those who are in Christ Jesus.

(Romans 8:1 NIV)

If we confess our sins, he is faithful and just and will forgive us our sins and purify us from all unrighteousness.

(1 John 1:9 NIV)

22But the fruit of the Spirit is love, joy, peace, forbearance, kindness, goodness, faithfulness, 23gentleness and self-control.

(Galatians 5:22-23a, NIV)

What You Will Need

- *Breakthrough* DVD and DVD player, or equipment to stream the video online
- Bible and *Breakthrough* participant workbook for reference
- Markerboard or chart paper and markers (optional)
- Stick-on name tags and markers (optional)
- iPod, smartphone, or tablet and portable speaker (optional)

Session Outline

Welcome and Opening Prayer (5-10 minutes, depending on session length)

In order to create a warm, welcoming environment as the women are gathering before the session begins, consider lighting one or more candles, providing coffee or other refreshments, and/or playing worship music. (Bring an iPod, smartphone, or tablet and a portable speaker if desired.) Be sure to provide nametags if the women do not know one another or you have new participants in your group. Then, when you are ready to begin, open the group in prayer.

If meeting online, welcome each participant as she joins and encourage the women to talk informally until you are ready to open the group in prayer.

Icebreaker (5 minutes)

Invite the women to share short responses to the following question:

- What do you think of when you hear the word *backsliding*?

Video (20 minutes)

Play the Week 5 video segment. Invite participants to complete the Video Viewer Guide for Week 5 in the participant workbook as they watch (page 173).

Group Discussion (25-35 minutes, depending on session length)

Note: More material is provided than you will have time to include. Before the session, select what you want to cover.

Video Discussion Questions
- What is the difference between practice and perfection?
- Have you ever tried to receive the fruit of the Spirit with your own will or effort? Have you noticed the fruit of the Spirit growing in you as a result of spending more time with God?
- What are some of the barriers to living in the Spirit?
- How can spiritual practices such as Bible study and prayer turn into legalistic hoops for us to jump through?

Participant Workbook Discussion Questions
1. While the gospel is what God has done to set us free, Paul calls us to remain free by standing firm. Standing firm isn't about holding on to our justification (right standing) or salvation in Christ. Rather, it aligns with sanctification, which is the process of becoming like Christ. We stand firm when we cooperate with what God is doing in our lives through intentionality and focus, making sure to guard against false messages and messengers. (Day 1)

   - What does standing firm look like for you? How do you stay intentional in what you listen to, read, or allow to influence your faith? (page 147)
   - What did you learn this week about justification and sanctification? What kinds of practices are tools that position you to allow God to do the work of sanctification in you?
   - Read Galatians 5:1. Why doesn't Paul want believers to get tied up in slavery to the law? (page 148) Have you ever known freedom and then found yourself bound up to something else at some point? If so, what was that like? Did you break free again, and if so, how?

2. Jesus didn't come to set us free because He wanted to shackle us or enslave us to His next agenda. That wouldn't have been freedom. He came to set us free so that we could stay free. (Day 1)

   • Read Matthew 23:2-4. What was Jesus's specific criticism of the Pharisees and teachers of the law? (page 149)
   • Read Matthew 11:28-30. What did Jesus say about His yoke? Knowing what you know about the law and the gospel, why is Jesus's yoke better than the yoke of following religious rules? (page 149)
   • How would you paraphrase Jesus's invitation to take on His yoke? What does it mean to you when you hear that invitation? What do you need to set down or take up in order to rest in the freedom granted you in Jesus?

3. Aside from the trap that the law would set for the Galatians, Paul knew that both legalism and license would rob them of the security and satisfaction of a loving, guilt-free relationship with God and others. The same goes for you and me. Living in God's love and showing God's love to others is the best version of freedom in Christ. (Day 2)

   • How do legalism and license rob us of a loving, guilt-free relationship with God? With others?
   • Read 1 Corinthians 10:23. Why do you think some Christians believe that because they are saved, they can act or live anyway they want to? (page 152) What are some examples of things that are lawful but not beneficial?
   • What are some of the spiritual and practical consequences of seeing the gospel as license to live any way that you want to? (page 152)
   • Review the story of the Good Samaritan (Luke 10:30-37). Why do you think the priest and the Levite passed by the injured man? As you reflect on this story and the people in your life who are hard to love, what are some takeaways for you? (page 154)

4. In the Book of Job in the Old Testament, Satan asks God for permission to devastate Job's life, and God allows it, confident in the character of Job. We can infer that what Satan means for evil, God will use for good (Genesis 50:20; Job 42). A similar dynamic may be in place with Paul. (Day 3)

- Read 2 Corinthians 12:8-9. What did God say was enough for Paul? What is/are the thorn(s) in your flesh? (page 156)
- Why do you think God allows some of our spiritual struggles to persist, even though we've tried to pray them away? (page 156)

5. When you allow God's Holy Spirit to guide your life, the promise is that you will find freedom from what your sinful nature (the flesh) desires or craves—freedom from your sin and strongholds. God's goal for your life isn't to make all of your problems go away. But when you allow the Spirit to fight for you, you'll experience victory. When you allow the Holy Spirit to guide your life, the result is holy living—even when there are occasional setbacks. Even when there are persistent pressures, seasonal resurgences, or surprise attacks, you can face them assured of ultimate victory in Jesus's name. (Day 3)

- Read Galatians 5:16. Who should guide our lives? What is the promise that comes with a Spirit-guided life? (page 156)
- Where might this promise bring fresh hope and perhaps even a breakthrough moment in your life? (page 157)
- Read John 14:26. How does the Holy Spirit guide our lives? (page 157)
- Read Galatians 5:17 and Romans 7:19. What is the tension that we face? (page 157) Think about an on-going, persistent struggle, sin, or stronghold in your life. How is it a spiritual battle and not a will-power issue? (page 158)
- When have you felt like you were being "stretched" spiritually? When have you felt that your stretching was bringing you closer to God? (page 158)

6. Because [those of us who struggle with legalism] try so hard to please God, we're spiritually crushed when it seems that we've failed. In fact, our spiritual failure, whether it's not doing our Bible study or missing church, makes us want to run and hide from God or double up on our To-Do, Do-More, and Do-Better actions to make up for it. But what if God doesn't care what we do when we fail, but instead cares more about whether we're willing to receive His mercy? Isn't that part of what the gospel is about? One of the most important distinctions in finding freedom from legalism is the difference between *conviction* and *condemnation*. Conviction connects us back to the gospel, whereas condemnation causes us to do even more or hide. (Day 4)

- How would you describe the difference between *conviction* and *condemnation*?
- Read Luke 18:13. What is the tax collector's prayer? How does his prayer resonate with your own heart?
- Read Luke 18:14. What did Jesus say about the outcome of the tax collector's prayer? Why was the tax collector, who had admitted to so many wrongs, sent home righteous whereas the Pharisee, who seemed to have done a lot right, went home unrighteous? (page 161) What do you think Jesus meant to show us with this example?
- Read 1 John 1:9 and Romans 8:1. What is the promise for those who confess their sins? What is the promise for those who are in Christ Jesus? (page 163) How do these promises lead you to breakthrough?

7. Realizing that the fruit of the Spirit is evidence of sanctification led to a breakthrough moment for me. I can use the fruit of the Spirit to discern whether I'm engaging in a spiritual discipline or activity because I'm trying to check off a to-do list (rules-oriented) or because I want to connect with or obey God (relationship-oriented). If I'm listening to worship music, serving others, giving, or reading my Bible because I want the Spirit to transform my character, that's good. But if I'm doing those things because I feel like I can gain points with God, that mindset needs to be challenged. (Day 5)

- Have you ever caught yourself doing something spiritual in order to impress God or others? If so, how did you discover that your motives were off?
- Can you recall an experience when you sensed that the Holy Spirit was working on one or more of the attributes of the fruit of the Spirit in your life? If so, describe it briefly. How did you cooperate with the Holy Spirit's work in your life? (page 168)
- Read Galatians 5:22-23. Why do you think Paul calls these nine attributes the fruit of the Spirit?
- Are there some spiritual struggles in your life that you can connect to the lack of certain attributes of the fruit of the Spirit? If so, what are they? How is the Spirit growing fruit in you?

Deeper Conversation (15 minutes)

Divide into smaller groups of 2-3 for deeper conversation. (Encourage the women to break into different groups each week.) If you'd like, before the session, write on a markerboard or chart paper the questions below. You could also do this in the form of a handout.

- Look at your ah-ha moments from the week and share about one of them.
- What spiritual breakthrough are you praying for right now?

Closing Prayer (5 minutes)

Close the session by taking personal prayer requests from group members and leading the group in prayer. Encourage members to participate by praying out loud for each other and the requests given.

Week 6

Forever Freedom

(Galatians 6)

Leader Prep (Before the Session)

Overview

In our last week of study, we focused on how the gospel gives us life, freedom, and confidence in our relationship with God and our relationships with others, particularly other believers. We were encouraged, inspired, and equipped to pursue healthy, whole, biblical relationships with others.

Throughout our study these past six weeks, Paul's teachings to the Galatians have reminded us of the power of the gospel in our lives each and every day. The gospel empowers us to walk in freedom in Christ so that we can live and love like Jesus and experience the great adventure of faith that God has for us. Our six freedom principles for the study are:

- The gospel is based on God's perfect promises, not our (or others') performance.
- A relationship with God means that we receive *from* Him rather than follow rules *for* Him.
- Freedom in Christ is living free from fear and fully alive with joy and purpose.
- Your freedom in Christ cannot be shaken or taken away by anyone who chooses not to live like Christ.
- Spiritual breakthrough is an ah-ha moment when we recognize that God is at work within us, receive what He's doing, and respond to it.
- You are God's beautiful, lovable, capable daughter. You are confident in Christ and worthy of God's best.

Freedom Principle #6

You are God's beautiful, lovable, capable daughter. You are confident in Christ and worthy of God's best.

Key Scriptures

May I never boast except in the cross of our Lord Jesus Christ, through which the world has been crucified to me, and I to the world.

(Galatians 6:14 NIV)

He comforts us in all our troubles so that we can comfort others. When they are troubled, we will be able to give them the same comfort God has given us.

(2 Corinthians 1:4)

Confess your sins to each other and pray for each other so that you may be healed. The earnest prayer of a righteous person has great power and produces wonderful results.

(James 5:16)

[7b] A man reaps what he sows. [8] Whoever sows to please their flesh, from the flesh will reap destruction; whoever sows to please the Spirit, from the Spirit will reap eternal life. [9] Let us not become weary in doing good, for at the proper time we will reap a harvest if we do not give up. [10] Therefore, as we have opportunity, let us do good to all people—especially to those who belong to the family of believers.

(Galatians 6:7b-10 NIV)

What You Will Need

- *Breakthrough* DVD and DVD player, or equipment to stream the video online
- Bible and *Breakthrough* participant workbook for reference
- Markerboard or chart paper and markers (optional)
- Stick-on name tags and markers (optional)
- iPod, smartphone, or tablet and portable speaker (optional)

Session Outline

Welcome and Opening Prayer (5-10 minutes, depending on session length)

In order to create a warm, welcoming environment as the women are gathering before the session begins, consider lighting one or more candles, providing coffee or other refreshments, and/or playing worship music. (Bring an iPod, smartphone, or tablet and a portable speaker if desired.) Be sure to provide nametags if the women do not know one another or you have new participants in your group. Then, when you are ready to begin, open the group in prayer.

If meeting online, welcome each participant as she joins and encourage the women to talk informally until you are ready to open the group in prayer.

Icebreaker (5 minutes)

Invite the women to share short responses to the following question:

- If you were to look back at your journals or diaries from 15-20 years ago, what would have been one fear that kept you from freedom?

Video (20 minutes)

Play the Week 6 video segment. Invite participants to complete the Video Viewer Guide for Week 6 in the participant workbook as they watch (page 204).

Group Discussion (25-35 minutes, depending on session length)

Note: More material is provided than you will have time to include. Before the session, select what you want to cover.

Video Discussion Questions
- Barb talked about having a line-in-the-sand moment about her finances. Have you had some line-in-the-sand moments in your life? What were they? How did they change your course?
- What is the difference between being prideful and being genuinely celebratory about a breakthrough?
- What are some ways to use our freedom to make a difference?
- What does it mean to reap a harvest of blessing? Have you ever had that experience?

Participant Workbook Discussion Questions
1. Unfortunately, we Christians often have the reputation of being inclined to judge and criticize instead of offer support when someone reveals an "emotional stone" or "sin stone" in his or her life. When Paul writes in Galatians 6 about restoring someone who's fallen into sin, the original language refers to how a physician resets a broken bone. If you've ever broken a bone, you know how painful it is. When a broken bone is unattended, it can still mend back together,

but the healing process takes much longer and the healed bone is often weaker than before. (Day 1)

- Why do you think Christians have a reputation for judging and criticizing? What are some ways to overcome that reputation and replace it with a reputation of grace?
- What are some examples of standing beside and supporting another believer who has fallen into sin? Include an example from your own life, if possible—whether you were the one who fell or the one who stood beside another. (page 177)
- Read Galatians 6:1. Is Paul's instruction directed to believers or nonbelievers? (page 176) At the end of verse 1, what is Paul's warning?

2. The best way to combat toxic church culture is to elevate the fruit of the Spirit in our individual and communal lives, especially when communicating with each other. (Day 1)

- How can allowing the fruit of the Spirit to lead our conversation help us to avoid toxic relationships and church culture? (page 178)
- Read Romans 2:4. How does God's kindness work in us? What lesson does that teach us about how we treat others who have fallen into sin?
- In your opinion, what are some reasons why Christians try to fix each other with rules or legalism instead of Spirit-led relationship? (page 179)

3. In Galatians 6:2, the Greek word "carry" is *bastazó*,[1] which means "to bear the physical, emotional or spiritual load threatening to crush his fellow believers."[2] Think about that for a moment. Paul isn't just telling believers that they are to sit politely across from someone over a cup of coffee. Rather, the imagery of the word *bastazó* seems to paint a picture of us contending with our hearts, minds, and souls for those who are caught in the trap of sin. (Day 2)

- Read Galatians 6:2. What are we to do for each other? What do you think carrying, sharing, or bearing our problems with each other has to do with the "law of Christ"? (page 183)

- Read James 5:16. What happens when we confess our sins to each other? What are some reasons that you or other Christians feel afraid or even embarrassed about sharing your struggles or sin? (page 185)
- Read Galatians 6:3-5. What message does Paul convey to those who feel they have it together? How have you compared the struggles and difficulties of your life or spiritual journey to others? How have those comparisons impacted your faith or how you feel about other Christians? (page 186)

4. If you've ever planned a garden, you know that whatever kind of seeds you put into the soil will grow. When you plant carrot seeds, you're going to get carrots, not onions. Onions will never grow from carrots. The same is true spiritually speaking. The fruit of the Spirit will never grow from works of the flesh. As we learn from Paul about how our freedom in Christ impacts our relationships with others, we need to recognize that our relationships are influenced by what we plant. (Day 3)

- How is your spiritual life like a garden that needs tending?
- Read Galatians 6:9. Why do you think doing good can be so tiring? What is the outcome of doing good, if we keep going? (page 191)
- Have you ever seen growth in a relationship directly related to how you tended it? What fruit showed up?

5. The Greek word for "good" is *kalos*, which means "attractive, inspires, motivates."[3] Of course, we want to produce that kind of outcome for God. Yet, it's really easy to shift from Spirit-led production into self-generated production. We cannot do God's good work on our own without God's power; if we try, we'll only burn out." (Day 3)

- Have you ever burned out trying to do good things for God? If so, describe it briefly. What are some factors that led to you getting burned out? (pages 191– 192)
- What are some signals in your heart and body that tell you when you're approaching burnout?
- What are some ways we can evaluate whether we're trying to produce our own fruit instead of letting God's good work grow fruit in us?

6. Because the Holy Spirit is at work in the life of every believer, our faith communities should be places where we're all cooperating with the Spirit's leadings. When we visualize the outcomes of the Gospel Wheel, our life together should be marked by stories of freedom, victory, purpose, and security. (Day 4)

   • Would you say your faith community is one where believers cooperate with the Spirit's leadings? Why or why not?
   • What does it mean to be in a community that might visualize the outcome of the Gospel Wheel?
   • What are some shared stories of your faith community related to freedom, victory, and purpose?

7. Beyond each of your spiritual breakthroughs is a greater expression of your freedom in Christ. As you live free from To-Do, Do-More, and Do-Better hoops and flow in the Gospel Wheel's cycle of freedom, victory, and purpose, you'll discover where and how the Spirit is leading you to live and love others better. Perhaps it's right in your own home by loving your family without imposing legalistic rules on them. Maybe it's an opportunity to lead a Bible study or other ministry team, nurturing other believers. Whatever you are led to do, your freedom in Christ will be a light that shines for God's glory! (Day 5)

   • In light of all that you've learned through this study, describe what it would look like for you to live fully in your freedom in Christ. (page 199)
   • What are three takeaways, verses, or stories from the letter to the Galatians that you want to remember? (page 200)
   • What are you most excited about on your new adventure in freedom, victory, and purpose?
   • Read Galatians 6:16-18. What is Paul's final prayer for the Galatians? (Refer to page 199.)

Deeper Conversation (15 minutes)

Divide into smaller groups of 2-3 for deeper conversation. (Encourage the women to break into different groups each week.) If you'd like, before the session, write on a markerboard or chart paper the questions below. You could also do this in the form of a handout.

- Look at your ah-ha moments over the last six weeks. Are there any that stand out to you? Are some more surprising than others? (page 202)
- How are you experiencing greater freedom in Christ after spending six weeks studying Paul's letter to the Galatians?
- Where do you still need God's freedom in your life? (page 202)

Closing Prayer (5 minutes)

Close the session by taking personal prayer requests from group members and leading the group in prayer. Encourage members to participate by praying out loud for each other and the requests given.

Video Viewer Guide
ANSWERS

Week 1
past / problems / pain
receiving / rules
To Do
Do More
Do Better
recognize / receive / respond
promises / performance

Week 2
mistakes
repents / resists
eyes
receive / rules

Week 3
transforms
transmits
transcends
shaken / taken

Week 4
released / reassigned
rules / free
power / presence
fear

Week 5
free / pressuring
practice / perfection
transformed
recognize / receive / respond

Week 6
acknowledge / celebrate
glory
confident / worthy

Notes

1. Bible Hub, s.v. "bastazó," https://biblehub.com/greek/941.htm.
2. E. Ray Clendenen and Jeremy Royal, eds., *Holman Illustrated Bible Commentary* (Nashville: B&H Publishing Group, 2015), 1275.
3. Bible Hub, s.v. "kalos," https://biblehub.com/greek/2570.htm.

Made in the USA
Middletown, DE
24 September 2024

61287223R00038